T0065199

A Matter of the Heart…

From the Soul of the Apostle/Preacher

+Dr. Sylvester Davis Johnson

Order this book online at www.trafford.com
or email orders@trafford.com

Most Trafford titles are also available at major online book retailers.

Print information available on the last page.

ISBN: 978-1-6987-1566-7 (sc)
ISBN: 978-1-6987-1567-4 (e)

Library of Congress Control Number: 2023920291

Scripture taken from the King James Version of the Bible.

Book Cover Design and Illustrations by
R.Charlestin Visual Media and Consulting

Trafford rev. 10/20/2023

 www.trafford.com
North America & international
toll-free: 844-688-6899 (USA & Canada)
fax: 812 355 4082

"The words of the Preacher, the son of David, king in Jerusalem."
Ecclesiastes 1:1 KJV

WORDS CANNOT SUFFICE TO THANK:

My All-Sufficient God (El-Shaddai):
For, daily, honoring my supplication to "orchestrate my life and give me the wisdom to perform the mandate that you set forth."

My wife, *"the fragrance of the house"* (Apostolic Manse, MWC, and every venue tier wherein we are pleasured to convene), First Lady, Co-Pastor, Bishop Billie Janetta Mason Johnson:
For your tolerance of my "Godly" hours of operation and unending "help-meet" undergirding in every aspect of my existence, "the protector of my heart".

The True Vine Churches of Deliverance International, affectionately known as (TVCOD):
The Greater Memorial Ecclesiastical Jurisdiction (GMEJ), A TVCOD Affiliate:
The Macedonia Worship Center (MWC):
For your years of impacting my life with sustenance, allegiance, and the lending of yourselves to an indelible "inspiration of my aspiration".

Bishop-Designate Dr. Reginald Meres Charlestin, Executive Administrator (locally, jurisdictionally, and internationally), Associate Pastor (MWC) Social-Networking Ministries (media, marketing, publication):
For your supportive efforts toward the completion of this publication.

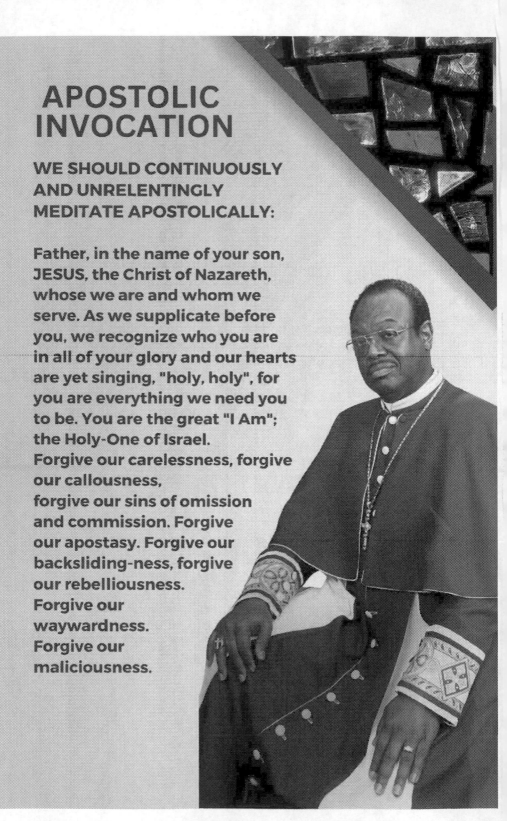

APOSTOLIC INVOCATION

WE SHOULD CONTINUOUSLY AND UNRELENTINGLY MEDITATE APOSTOLICALLY:

Father, in the name of your son, JESUS, the Christ of Nazareth, whose we are and whom we serve. As we supplicate before you, we recognize who you are in all of your glory and our hearts are yet singing, "holy, holy", for you are everything we need you to be. You are the great "I Am"; the Holy-One of Israel. Forgive our carelessness, forgive our callousness, forgive our sins of omission and commission. Forgive our apostasy. Forgive our backsliding-ness, forgive our rebelliousness. Forgive our waywardness. Forgive our maliciousness.

Deliver us from the cesspool of degradation, deprivation, and desecration. Deliver us from animosity, iniquity, and guile. Deliver us from disgrace to "amazing grace". Deliver us from the muddy waters of egomania.

Deliver us from the "onslaught of the slaughterer." Deliver us from the gainsayers, the naysayers, the doomsayers, and the soothsayers who come to inundate us with intimidation, bigotry, and demagoguery Deliver us from the isms and schisms of denominationalism.

Make us to hear joy and gladness that the bones which thou hast broken may rejoice. Elevate us into a new dimension of reconciliation, rectification, justification, sanctification, manifestation, and celebration as we hear the clarion call for repentance and the return to apostolic excellence.

So, help us to rise above the status quo or business-as-usual going forward as only you can forgive and release us with righteousness that glorifies Him. We are grateful for the global challenge as we speak life to the nations and over every governmental official and hierarchy.

Bless this time of apostolic salutation, declaration, and impartation. Cause us to understand that we are more impactful together than we are independently separate and apart.

This we declare in Jesus's precious name and to His name's glory, world, without end...Amen.

A Matter of the Heart…

From the Soul of the Apostle/Preacher

EVERY DAY, WHEN WE AWAKEN,
WE SHOULD HAVE A GODLY
AWARENESS THAT:

*"THIS IS THE DAY WHICH THE
LORD HATH MADE; WE WILL
REJOICE AND BE GLAD IN IT."*
PSALM 118:24 KJV

THIS DAY...SO FILLED WITH
OPPORTUNITIES AND
POSSIBILITIES,
"DREAM FULFILLMENT" AND
"VISION MANIFESTATION".

THIS DAY...WHEREIN WE ARE
CONSCIOUS OF THE FACT THAT IT
IS DULY AND TRULY:

GOD-GIVEN
GOD-GLADDENED
GOD-GOVERNED

THEREFORE; WE PRAYERFULLY
AND INDIVIDUALLY WELCOME
HIM TO "ORCHESTRATE OUR
LIVES" AND "GIVE US THE
WISDOM TO PERFORM THE
MANDATE THAT HE SETS FORTH".

*"IF ANY OF YOU LACK WISDOM,
LET HIM ASK OF GOD, THAT
GIVETH TO ALL MEN LIBERALLY,
AND UPBRAIDETH NOT; AND IT
SHALL BE GIVEN HIM."
JAMES 1:5 KJV*

Reflections

"Humble yourselves therefore under the mighty hand of God, that he may exalt you in due time:"
1 Peter 5:6 KJV

GIVE GOD THE ROOM HE NEEDS TO EXALT YOU BY GETTING IN THE POSTURE OF HUMILITY (YIELDED AND STILL).

> " Don't get lost in someone you call "influential". Work the works of Him who have sent you. What is the Lord pouring into you? What's in your character that God can use? God did not call you to be anyone else. You have to admire the God-man that is within you. And be around somebody who will constantly push out the YOU in YOU. "

-APOSTLE DR. SYLVESTER DAVIS JOHNSON
"Spiritual Father/Son Relationship Impacting the Kingdom of God"
TVCOD "To Protect & Serve" Virtual Symposium 2023

GOD DOES NOT MERELY REQUIRE OUR BEST,
HE REQUIRES OUR "ALL"!

IS YOUR "ALL" ON THE "ALTAR OF SACRIFICE"
LAID; YOUR HEART, DOTH THE SPIRIT CONTROL?
YOU CAN ONLY BE BLEST AND FIND PEACE AND
SWEET REST, AS YOU YIELD HIM YOUR BODY
AND SOUL.

*"TRUST IN THE LORD WITH ALL THINE HEART;
AND LEAN NOT UNTO THINE OWN
UNDERSTANDING. IN ALL THY WAYS
ACKNOWLEDGE HIM, AND HE SHALL DIRECT THY
PATHS." PROVERBS 3:5-6 KJV*

YIELDING CREATES A SUPERNATURAL
RENAISSANCE:

SPECIAL SPIRITUAL MIRACLES

SPECIAL PHYSICAL MIRACLES

SPECIAL FINANCIAL MIRACLES

SPECIAL MENTAL/EMOTIONAL MIRACLES

*"AND GOD WROUGHT SPECIAL MIRACLES BY THE
HANDS OF PAUL: SO THAT FROM HIS BODY WERE
BROUGHT UNTO THE SICK HANDKERCHIEFS OR
APRONS, AND THE DISEASES DEPARTED FROM
THEM, AND THE EVIL SPIRITS WENT OUT OF
THEM."
ACTS 19:11-12 KJV*

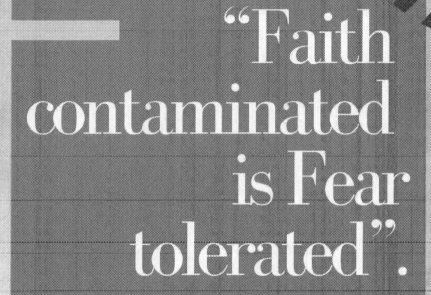

"Faith contaminated is Fear tolerated".

"Now faith is the substance of things hoped for, the evidence of things not seen."
Hebrews 11:1. KJV

GOD, LITERALLY, GIVES US TIME AND THE WHEREWITHAL TO MAKE DECISIONS, THAT WILL DETERMINE OUR DESTINY, THIS IS A "PIVOTAL MOMENT;" ALLOW IT TO BE AN "EPIPHANY MOMENT".

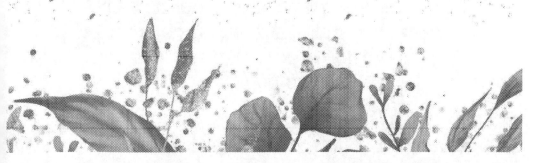

Have I conceived all this people? have I begotten them, that thou shouldest say unto me, Carry them in thy bosom, as a nursing father beareth the sucking child, unto the land which thou swarest unto their fathers? Whence should I have flesh to give unto all this people? for they weep unto me, saying, Give us flesh, that we may eat. I am not able to bear all this people alone, because it is too heavy for me. And if thou deal thus with me, kill me, I pray thee, out of hand, if I have found favour in thy sight; and let me not see my wretchedness. And the LORD said unto Moses, Gather unto me seventy men of the elders of Israel, whom thou knowest to be the elders of the people, and officers over them; and bring them unto the tabernacle of the congregation, that they may stand there with thee. And I will come down and talk with thee there: and I will take of the spirit which is upon thee, and will put it upon them; and they shall bear the burden of the people with thee, that thou bear it not thyself alone. And say thou unto the people, Sanctify yourselves against to morrow, and ye shall eat flesh: for ye have wept in the ears of the LORD, saying, Who shall give us flesh to eat? for it was well with us in Egypt: therefore the LORD will give you flesh, and ye shall eat. Ye shall not eat one day, nor two days, nor five days, neither ten days, nor twenty days; but even a whole month, until it come out at your nostrils, and it be loathsome unto you: because that ye have despised the LORD which is among you, and have wept before him, saying, Why came we forth out of Egypt?"

Numbers 11:12-20 KJV

APOSTOLIC LEADERSHIP ACCOUNTABILITY IS TO GOD; NOT MAN; THEREFORE, HE SURROUNDS HIMSELF WITH ASTUTE, DEDICATED, DIGNIFIED, AND DISCIPLINED SUBORDINATE LEADERSHIP - THOSE WHO ARE ENDOWED WITH UNQUESTIONABLE BUSINESS ACUMEN, WHO CAN HELP HIM WITH HIS ACCOUNTABILITY TO "GOD": "F-A-T SUBORDINATES WHO ARE "FAITHFUL", "ACCOUNTABLE" AND "TEACHABLE" AT ALL TIMES. THIS IS THE "TYPOLOGY OF A MARRIAGE" WHEREIN THE WOMAN BECOMES "HER HUSBAND'S HELPMEET" AND IS CHARGED TO "GUARD HIS HEART", IN HIS ROLE AS HER COVERING.

WE SALUTE THOSE
IN EVERY TIER OF
LEADERSHIP, IN
THE CHURCH,
WHO HAVE
DISTINGUISHED
THEMSELVES AS
"F-A-T" -
"FAITHFUL,
ACCOUNTABLE;
TEACHABLE"
SERVANT-
LEADERS.

"And it shall come to pass in the last days, that the mountain of the LORD 's house shall be established in the top of the mountains, and shall be exalted above the hills; and all nations shall flow unto it. And many people shall go and say, Come ye, and let us go up to the mountain of the LORD, to the house of the God of Jacob; and he will teach us of his ways, and we will walk in his paths: for out of Zion shall go forth the law, and the word of the LORD from Jerusalem."
Isaiah 2:2-3 KJV

THE APOSTLES ARE GATHERING THE NATIONS FOR A "MOUNTAIN-TOP EXPERIENCE".

THE CRESCENDO RISES AS THEY PROGRESS:

"They go from strength to strength, Every one of them in Zion appeareth before God." Psalm 84:7 KJV

"And he gave some, apostles; and some, prophets; and some, evangelists; and some, pastors and teachers; for the perfecting of the saints, for the work of the ministry, for the edifying of the body of Christ: till we all come in the unity of the faith, and of the knowledge of the Son of God, unto a perfect man, unto the measure of the stature of the fulness of Christ: that we henceforth be no more children, tossed to and fro, and carried about with every wind of doctrine, by the sleight of men, and cunning craftiness, whereby they lie in wait to deceive; but speaking the truth in love, may grow up into him in all things, which is the head, even Christ: from whom the whole body fitly joined together and compacted by that which every joint supplieth, according to the effectual working in the measure of every part, maketh increase of the body unto the edifying of itself in love."

Ephesians 4:11-16 KJV

THEREFORE, THE FIVE (5)-FOLD MINISTRY IS GOD'S GIFTING TO HIS BODY, HIS CHURCH; HIS "BAPTIZED BELIEVERS IN CHRIST".
SUPPORT THEM IN THEIR DEFINITIVE ROLES:

THE APOSTLE GOVERNS
THE PROPHET GUIDES
THE EVANGELIST GATHERS
THE PASTOR GUARDS
THE TEACHER GROUNDS
SUPPLICATE WITH THEM ALWAYS!

"WHOSE KINGDOM IS IT ANYWAY?"

"For thine is the kingdom, and the power, and the glory, for ever. Amen."

WHO IS THIS MAN CALLED JESUS?

THE CENTRAL IDEA OF OUR MESSAGE WILL SET FORTH THE FACT(NOT A THEORY; NOT A POSTULATE)THAT:

JESUS DIED AS A SAVIOR. AND ROSE AS A KING; BECAUSE EVERY CHURCH NEEDS A SAVIOR AND EVERY KINGDOM NEEDS A KING !

Jesus taught His disciples how to conduct themselves with the tenets of almsgiving, prayer and fasting:

Matthew 6:9-15

"After this manner therefore pray ye: Our Father which art in heaven, Hallowed be thy name. Thy kingdom come. Thy will be done in earth, as it is in heaven. Give us this day our daily bread. And forgive us our debts, as we forgive our debtors. And lead us not into temptation, but deliver us from evil: For thine is the kingdom, and the power, and the glory, for ever. Amen.

For if ye forgive men their trespasses, your heavenly Father will also forgive you: but if ye forgive not men their trespasses, neither will your Father forgive your trespasses."
Matthew 6:9-15 KJV

I.) FIRSTLY, WHOSE KINGDOM IS IT ANYWAY?

Jesus' kingdom is solidified - FOR EVERY KINGDOM HAS A KING

Matthew 16:13-19
"When Jesus came into the coasts of Cæsarea Philippi, he asked his disciples, saying, Whom do men say that I the Son of man am? And they said, Some say that thou art John the Baptist: some, Elias; and others, Jeremias, or one of the prophets. He saith unto them, But whom say ye that I am? And Simon Peter answered and said, Thou art the Christ, the Son of the living God. And Jesus answered and said unto him, Blessed art thou, Simon Bar-jona: for flesh and blood hath not revealed it unto thee, but my Father which is in heaven.

And I say also unto thee, That thou art Peter, and upon this rock I will build my church; and the gates of hell shall not prevail against it. And I will give unto thee the keys of the kingdom of heaven: and whatsoever thou shalt bind on earth shall be bound in heaven: and whatsoever thou shalt loose on earth shall be loosed in heaven."
Matthew 16:13-19 KJV

II.) SECONDLY, WHOSE KINGDOM IS IT ANYWAY?

When Jesus was here in the world there were many, many tasks; many jobs that he entrusted into the hands of men. Before His Ascension, Jesus trusted men to preach, trusted them to teach, trusted them to baptize; he even trusted men to lay on hands. But when it came to the building, the erecting, the constructing of his church, he said, "I will build my church."

THE HEADQUARTERS OF MY KINGDOM; NOT AN ISLAMIC MOSQUE, NOT A BUDDHIST MONASTERY, NOT A KINGDOM HALL

The construction of the church was too tedious for him to entrust into the hands of imperfect men; therefore, he was very selfish about it, "I will build my church."

- Not Peter; for if I were to allow Peter to build it, I would have a "denying church"

- Not Thomas; for if I were to allow Thomas to build it, I would have a "doubting church"

- Not Matthew; for if I were to allow Matthew to build it, I would have a "cheating church"

- Not Judas; for if I were to allow Judas to build it, I would have a "betraying church"

- Not the other disciples; for if I were to allow the other disciples to build it, I would have a "retreating church"

III.) THIRDLY, WHOSE KINGDOM IS IT ANYWAY?

Search the pages of the holy writ and you will find that when Jesus was here the little personal pronoun "my" was always a word that Jesus used with great reservation and strictness. Search the pages of the four(4) gospels and not often will you find that Jesus used the word, "my". The only thing that he thought about that was close enough to him to use "my" was his father, his disciples, his church - my father, my disciples, my church (my house shall be called a house of prayer, but you have made it a den of thieves).

VI.) FOURTHLY AND LASTLY, WHOSE KINGDOM IS IT ANYWAY?

John1:1-14
In the beginning was the Word, and the Word was with God, and the Word was God. The same was in the beginning with God. All things were made by him; and without him was not any thing made that was made. In him was life; and the life was the light of men.

III.) THIRDLY, WHOSE KINGDOM IS IT ANYWAY?

Search the pages of the holy writ and you will find that when Jesus was here the little personal pronoun "my" was always a word that Jesus used with great reservation and strictness. Search the pages of the four(4) gospels and not often will you find that Jesus used the word, "my". The only thing that he thought about that was close enough to him to use "my" was his father, his disciples, his church - my father, my disciples, my church (my house shall be called a house of prayer, but you have made it a den of thieves).

VI.) FOURTHLY AND LASTLY, WHOSE KINGDOM IS IT ANYWAY?

John1:1-14
In the beginning was the Word, and the Word was with God, and the Word was God. The same was in the beginning with God. All things were made by him; and without him was not any thing made that was made. In him was life; and the life was the light of men.

And the light shineth in darkness; and the darkness comprehended it not. There was a man sent from God, whose name was John. The same came for a witness, to bear witness of the Light, that all men through him might believe. He was not that Light, but was sent to bear witness of that Light (he was the HARBINGER- a fore-runner of something. A person or thing that announces or signals the approach of another). That was the true Light, which lighteth every man that cometh into the world. He was in the world, and the world was made by him, and the world knew him not. He came unto his own, and his own received him not. But as many as received him, to them gave he power to become the sons of God, even to them that believe on his name: Which were born, not of blood, nor of the will of the flesh, nor of the will of man, but of God. And the Word was made flesh, and dwelt among us, (and we beheld his glory, the glory as of the only begotten of the Father,) full of grace and truth. (John 1:1-14 KJV)

"Let this mind be in you, which was also in Christ Jesus: who, being in the form of God, thought it not robbery to be equal with God: but made himself of no reputation, and took upon him the form of a servant, and was made in the likeness of men: and being found in fashion as a man, he humbled himself, and became obedient unto death, even the death of the cross. Wherefore God also hath highly exalted him, and given him a name which is above every name: that at the name of Jesus every knee should bow, of things in heaven, and things in earth, and things under the earth; and that every tongue should confess that Jesus Christ is Lord, to the glory of God the Father."

Philippians 2:5-11 KJV

JESUS IS VERY GOD:

- GOD WITH US AT BETHLEHEM
- GOD FOR US AT CALVARY
- GOD IN US AT PENTECOST
- KING OF KINGS; LORD OF LORDS...

OUR FATHER, GOD, ENDOWS US WITH THE "MENTAL ACUMEN" - "KEENNESS AND DEPTH OF PERCEPTION, DISCERNMENT OR DISCRIMINATION; ESPECIALLY IN PRACTICAL MATTERS" TO EXERCISE "STRATEGIC PLANNING"; THUSLY ASSURING:

*MOBILITY, MOMENTUM, MOTIVATION
*FAITHFULNESS, FRUITFULNESS (FERTILITY), FUTURE
*CORDIALITY, CONGENIALITY, CHARISMA

"IF YOU CANNOT FLY THEN RUN,
IF YOU CANNOT RUN THEN WALK,
IF YOU CANNOT WALK THEN CRAWL,
BUT WHATEVER YOU DO, YOU'VE GOT TO KEEP MOVING."
-REV. DR. MARTIN LUTHER KING, JR.-

THE APOSTLE IS PURPOSELY
DESTINED, BY THE GRACE OF GOD,
TO "REACH THE MASSES" AND
EFFECT CHANGE THAT DELIVERS
FROM:
FRAGMENTATION TO WHOLENESS
SICKNESS TO WELLNESS
ILLITERACY TO LITERACY
FEAR TO BOLDNESS
DOUBT TO FAITH
DAMNATION TO SALVATION
DISGRACE TO "AMAZING GRACE"
...AND A PLETHORA OF
CATEGORIES AS NEEDED.
PLEASE PARTICIPATE IN THE
PROCESS OF "REACHING THE LOST
AT ANY COST THROUGH
PENTECOST".

You can not incite worship. It must be induced by Holy Spirit.

"Worship Undergirded by Holy Spirit"
John 4:23-24, KJV

"Even the youths shall faint and be weary, and the young men shall utterly fall: but they that wait upon the LORD shall renew their strength; they shall mount up with wings as eagles; they shall run, and not be weary; and they shall walk, and not faint."
Isaiah 40:30-31 KJV

YOU HAVE BEEN WAITING PATIENTLY ON THE "PERSEVERANCE LAUNCHING PAD" FOR. THE "TAKE -OFF" AND "MOUNT-UP", FOR "RENEWED STRENGTH", "THE SET-TIME IS COME:"

"Thou shalt arise, and have mercy upon Zion: For the time to favour her, yea, the set time, is come."
Psalm 102:13 KJV

"ELEVATE YOUR MIND AND LET'S GO HIGHER CONTINUALLY"

GOD HAS SO "GRACIOUSLY" "WONDROUSLY" AND "OVERLY" ENDOWED ME WITH AN "OVER-FLOWING" JOY, UNSPEAKABLE, AND FULL OF GLORY!

"Blessed be the God and Father of our Lord Jesus Christ, which according to his abundant mercy hath begotten us again unto a lively hope by the resurrection of Jesus Christ from the dead, to an inheritance incorruptible, and undefiled, and that fadeth not away, reserved in heaven for you, who are kept by the power of God through faith unto salvation ready to be revealed in the last time. Wherein ye greatly rejoice, though now for a season, if need be, ye are in heaviness through manifold temptations: that the trial of your faith, being much more precious than of gold that perisheth, though it be tried with fire, might be found unto praise and honour and glory at the appearing of Jesus Christ: whom having not seen, ye love; in whom, though now ye see him not, yet believing, ye rejoice with joy unspeakable and full of glory:"
1 Peter 1:3-8 KJV

" Thou anointest my head with oil; my cup runneth over."
Psalm 23:5b KJV

ON A "JOY SCALE" FROM 1-10, I AM "TIPPING" THE SCALE AT 15: "5" IS THE NUMBER OF GRACE
"10" IS DOUBLE-GRACE
"15" IS TRIPLE GRACE

THE APOSTLE IS INNATELY
DRIVEN TO ENCAPSULATE "THE
BODY OF CHRIST" WITHIN A
CAPSULE OF "METHOD" THAT
DIMINISHES "MADNESS".

HE DOES IT WITH "BODACIOUS
INTENTIONALITY AND PURPOSE"
WHICH ASSURES THAT THE PEOPLE
ARE BLESSED AND THAT GOD IS
DULY AND TRULY GLORIFIED.
"SO HELP US, GOD".

GOD IS DELIVERING, NOW, FROM THE QUAGMIRE OF RESTLESSNESS AND HOPELESSNESS; FROM THE MENTAL ANGUISH OF ANXIETY AND DEPRESSION!

"HE SENT HIS WORD, AND HEALED THEM, AND DELIVERED THEM FROM THEIR DESTRUCTIONS."
PSALM 107:20 KJV

"This is the day which the LORD hath made; We will rejoice and be glad in it."
Psalm 118:24 KJV

"T-H-I-S D-A-Y" (era, time)
- GOD-GIVEN
- GOD-GLADDENED
- GOD-GOVERNED

SO FILLED WITH:
- OPPORTUNITIES; POSSIBILITIES
- DREAM FULFILLMENT;
VISION MANIFESTATION
- MIRACLES, SIGNS; WONDERS

It is imperative that we seek Him daily for the orchestration of our personal lives and undertakings; therefore, we must, personally, offer our supplication for wisdom to enact the mandate that He sets forth.

"Let us therefore come boldly unto the throne of grace, that we may obtain mercy, and find grace to help in time of need."
Hebrews 4:16 KJV.

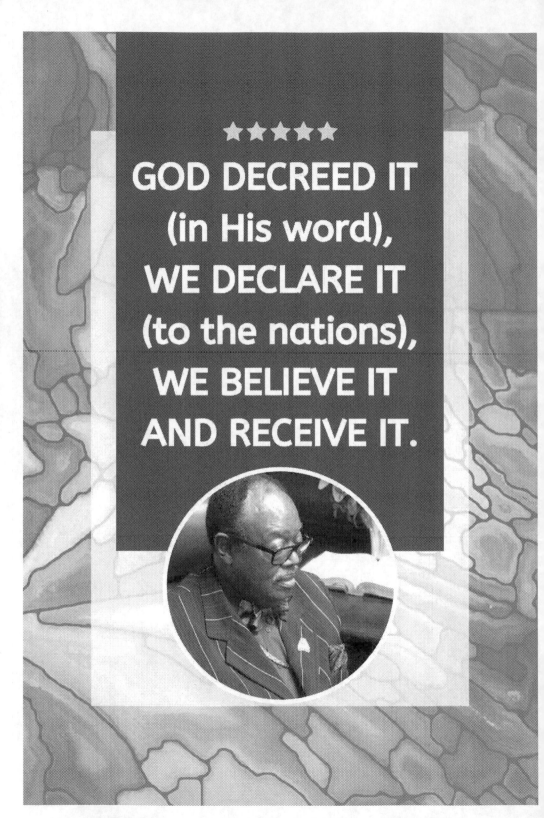

GOD DECREED IT
(in His word),
WE DECLARE IT
(to the nations),
WE BELIEVE IT
AND RECEIVE IT.

> "Iron sharpeneth iron; So a man sharpeneth the countenance of his friend."
> Proverbs 27:17 KJV

WHEN APOSTLES UNITE, "SHOULDER-TO-SHOULDER", COUNTENANCES BECOME SHARPER BECAUSE OF THE GENUINE; LUCID NETWORKING. VISION BECOMES CLEARER. WE ARE MORE IMPACTFUL TOGETHER!

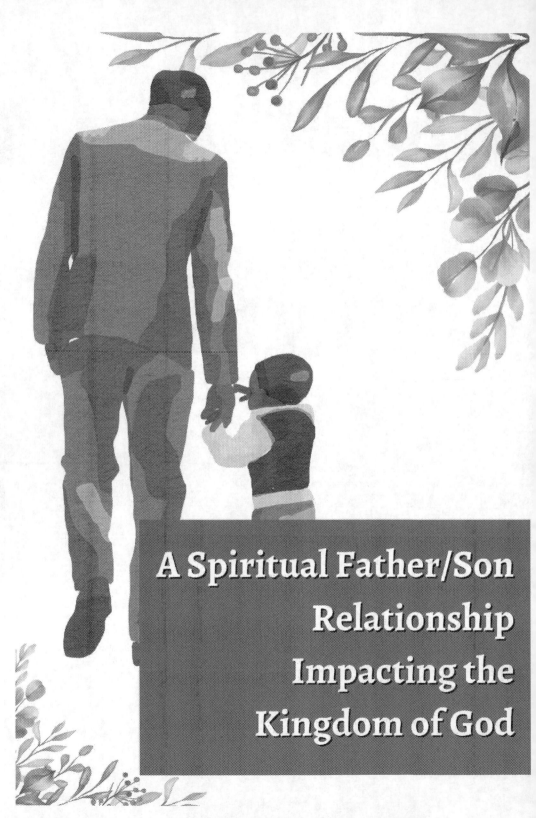

A Spiritual Father/Son
Relationship
Impacting the
Kingdom of God

SCRIPTURAL REFERENCE:
A son honoureth his father, and a
servant his master: if then I be a
father, where is mine honour? and if I
be a master, where is my fear? saith
the Lord of hosts unto you, O priests,
that despise my name. And ye say,
Wherein have we despised thy name?
(Malachi 1:6 KJV)

Longevity in any aspect of ministry
will cause you to understand that:
When men set themselves to degrade,
denounce and demean you, they have
an inbred, insatiable "demonic
commitment to debauchery" to belittle
you and reduce you to

"the least common denominator" of disgrace, so as to "rail your reputation", in an effort to "derail your destiny."

2 Corinthians 2:10
To whom ye forgive any thing, I forgive also: for if I forgave any thing, to whom I forgave it, for your sakes forgave I it in the person of Christ; Lest Satan should get an advantage of us: for we are not ignorant of his devices. Furthermore, when I came to Troas to preach Christ's gospel, and a door was opened unto me of the Lord, I had no rest in my spirit, because I found not Titus my brother: but taking my leave of them, I went from

thence into Macedonia. Now thanks be unto God, which always causeth us to triumph in Christ, and maketh manifest the savour of his knowledge by us in every place. (2 Corinthians 2:10-14 KJV)

A Spiritual Father/Son Relationship Impacting the Kingdom of God

Within the spiritual father dwells a spirit of mentoring. The spiritual son maintains a spirit of reverent submission; thusly, causing him to be a protégé.

- Protégé – a man under the care and protection (covering) of an influential person usually for the furthering of his career
- Mentor – a trusted counselor or guide, tutor, or coach whom you esteem highly

"The passion of the protégé is revealed by his pursuit of the mentor."

-Mike Murdoch

His passion is coupled with compassion to the extent that he will not comfortably degrade, downplay or misalign their relationship causing the covering to be blown.

He understands that tearing down the influence of the influential will only cause the relationship to be stymied. He understands that "those who have what you don't have, know what you don't know." His passion for ministry and the furtherance of the kingdom is revealed by the pursuit of that knowledge.

Elisha pursued Elijah for his mantle (II King 2:9); however, in this New Testament dispensation, the spiritual father is aware of the fact that the spiritual son has a calling upon his life and must work the works of the heavenly Father who sent him. Jesus makes it explicitly clear that I "must work the works of Him that sent me;"

• My meat is to do the will of Him that
sent me and to finish His work
(St. John 4:34)

• I told you, and ye believed not: the
works that I do in my Father's name,
they bear witness of me
(St. John 10:25)

• For I have given unto them the words
which thou gavest me: and they have
received them and have known surely
that I came out from thee, and they
have believed that thou didst send me
(St. John 17:8)

So it is, the spiritual father understands that his role as a mentor is one of motivating his spiritual son to heights unknown. He is the recipient of great joy when a son sits at his feet as Paul sat at the feet of Gamaliel – in the quest for knowledge. He takes pride in seeing his spiritual son grow in the grace and knowledge of our Lord and Savior, Jesus Christ.

Every profession has unethical and, consequently, churchdom has some as well. Our pulpits are littered with those who have not waited upon their calling; those who have not waited upon their ministry; "those who were not sent, they just went." This is a serious affront to God's Holy Ecclesia. Renegades are in overwhelming proportion simply because they view the pulpit as a place of glamour. They fail to realize that:

• Untutored wonders are becoming blunders
• Uncovered grand leaders are being grounded
• Un-nurtured "deep neophytes" are being buried in the muddy waters of egomania

Therefore, it becomes questionable as to who really sent us, Jesus makes it clear that if we cannot believe the words of God, we cannot do His works impactfully.

The character of a spiritual father/son relationship is one of covenant fellowship and respect. For when we do not stay in character, we cannot make access to the vast highway of Holiness in God's Kingdom, somewhat like our personal computers where we are allowed a screen name and a password. We are given the privilege of selecting characters with combinations of letters and numbers which gives us the right to access the World Wide

Web (www). Anytime we fail to use the designated characters, we are denied access to the internet.

So it is, if we do not abide by our designated callings; if we do not stay in character, we are denied access to the anointing of God which causes us to be able ministers in His Kingdom. Therefore, motivation in the spiritual father/son relationship becomes an aspect of reciprocity ("giving and receiving") as we forge ahead in accordance with Ephesians 4:11-16:

And he gave some, apostles; and some, prophets; and some, evangelists; and some, pastors and teachers; For the perfecting of the saints, for the work of the ministry, for the edifying of the body of Christ: Till we all come in the unity of the faith, and of the knowledge of the Son of God, unto a perfect man, unto the measure of the stature of the fullness of Christ: That we henceforth be no more children, tossed to and fro, and carried about with every wind of doctrine, by the sleight of men, and cunning craftiness, whereby they lie in wait to deceive; But speaking the truth in love, may grow up into him in all things, which is the head, even

Christ: From whom the whole body fitly joined together and compacted by that which every joint supplieth, according to the effectual working in the measure of every part, maketh increase of the body unto the edifying of itself in love.

Finally, the spiritual paradigm of the father/son relationship is most impactful upon the Kingdom of God when our parishioners can visibly interpret our mannerism as SINCERE INTERACTION; thereby spiritually inciting them to PARTICIPATE PROACTIVELY in our quest for covenant fellowship locally, nationally, and globally.

They will know us by our love.

By Apostle Sylvester Davis Johnson,
The Most Apostolic Primate/Establishmentarian of
The True Vine Churches of Deliverance International,
Contributing Writer to Vision Magazine
– April/May 2010 Inaugural Issue

WITHIN CHRISTENDOM AND CHURCHDOM, WE SHOULD SEEK TO OPERATE WITHIN THE BOUNDARY OF "PEACE" - THAT PASSETH ALL UNDERSTANDING WHICH PRODUCES "CALMNESS, SERENITY AND TRANQUILITY".

"And the peace of God, which passeth all understanding, shall keep your hearts and minds through Christ Jesus."

Philippians 4:7 KJV

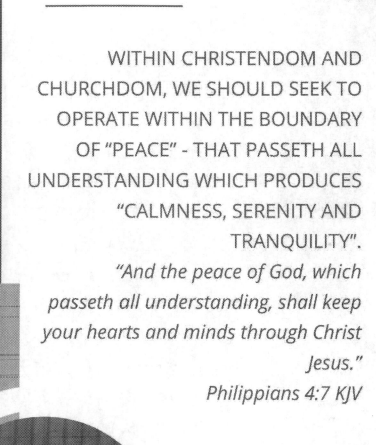

THEREFORE, WE SHOULD, EVER, BE
REMINDED OF THE "DEBILITATING" -
"IMPAIRMENT OF STRENGTH OR
ABILITY TO FUNCTION" WHICH IS
THE CONSEQUENTIAL EFFECT OF
CONFUSION AND DISHARMONY:
*"But if ye bite and devour one
another, take heed that ye be not
consumed one of another. This I say
then, Walk in the Spirit, and ye shall
not fulfil the lust of the flesh. For the
flesh lusteth against the Spirit, and the
Spirit against the flesh: and these are
contrary the one to the other: so that
ye cannot do the things that ye would."*
Galatians 5:15-17 KJV

WE MUST "CONSECRATE OURSELVES" - "THROUGH FASTING AND PRAYERS", WITHOUT CEASING: *"Is not this the fast that I have chosen? to loose the bands of wickedness, to undo the heavy burdens, and to let the oppressed go free, and that ye break every yoke?"* *Isaiah 58:6 KJV*

NOW IS THE SET TIME TO OFFER PRAYERS OF "SUPPLICATION" - WHEREIN WE "IMPLORE AND PETITION GOD", SINCERELY, "TO CALM EVERY DOUBT, FEAR AND APPREHENSION"; AND "TO REBUKE EVERY FOE, WOE AND HINDRANCE" TO OUR HARMONIOUS RELATIONSHIPS.

"Woe unto the world because of offenses! for it must needs be that offenses come; but woe to that man by whom the offense cometh!"
Matthew 18:7 KJV

"DO NOT CONTINUE TO WALK IN OFFENSES"

"BE HEALED, BE DELIVERED, BE SET FREE, NOW"

"When we
see Him our
lives are changed.
When we see Him our
lives are enhanced. This
is why worship is
important. My life has
been made better
because of worship."

"See Jesus and Go Home Another Way"
Matthew 2:1-12, KJV

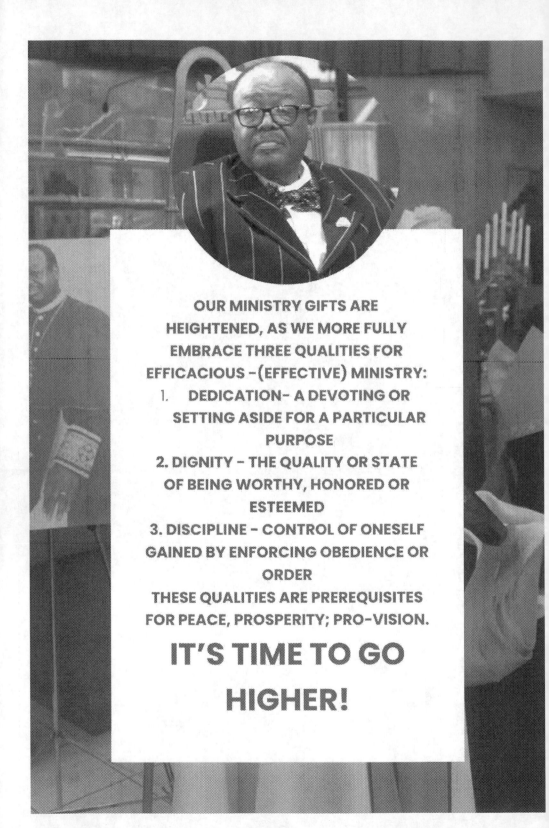

OUR MINISTRY GIFTS ARE
HEIGHTENED, AS WE MORE FULLY
EMBRACE THREE QUALITIES FOR
EFFICACIOUS -(EFFECTIVE) MINISTRY:

1. DEDICATION- A DEVOTING OR
   SETTING ASIDE FOR A PARTICULAR
   PURPOSE
2. DIGNITY - THE QUALITY OR STATE
   OF BEING WORTHY, HONORED OR
   ESTEEMED
3. DISCIPLINE - CONTROL OF ONESELF
   GAINED BY ENFORCING OBEDIENCE OR
   ORDER

THESE QUALITIES ARE PREREQUISITES
FOR PEACE, PROSPERITY; PRO-VISION.

IT'S TIME TO GO
HIGHER!

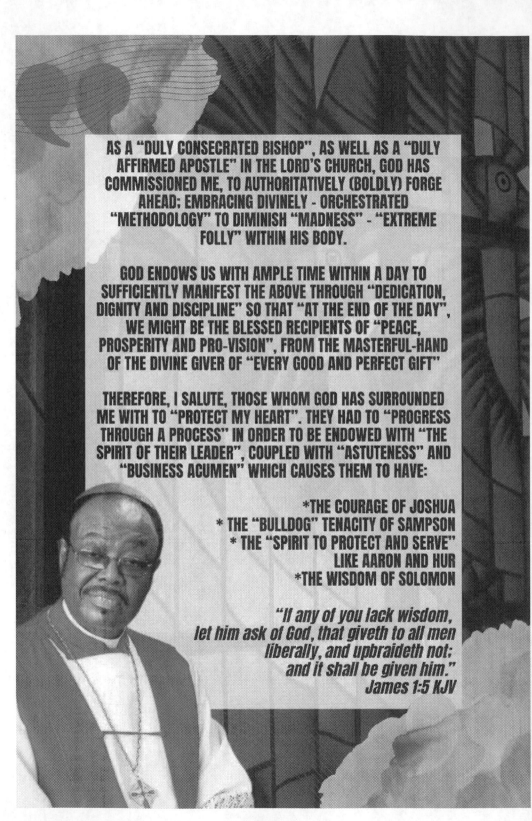

AS A "DULY CONSECRATED BISHOP", AS WELL AS A "DULY AFFIRMED APOSTLE" IN THE LORD'S CHURCH, GOD HAS COMMISSIONED ME, TO AUTHORITATIVELY (BOLDLY) FORGE AHEAD; EMBRACING DIVINELY - ORCHESTRATED "METHODOLOGY" TO DIMINISH "MADNESS" - "EXTREME FOLLY" WITHIN HIS BODY.

GOD ENDOWS US WITH AMPLE TIME WITHIN A DAY TO SUFFICIENTLY MANIFEST THE ABOVE THROUGH "DEDICATION, DIGNITY AND DISCIPLINE" SO THAT "AT THE END OF THE DAY", WE MIGHT BE THE BLESSED RECIPIENTS OF "PEACE, PROSPERITY AND PRO-VISION", FROM THE MASTERFUL-HAND OF THE DIVINE GIVER OF "EVERY GOOD AND PERFECT GIFT"

THEREFORE, I SALUTE, THOSE WHOM GOD HAS SURROUNDED ME WITH TO "PROTECT MY HEART". THEY HAD TO "PROGRESS THROUGH A PROCESS" IN ORDER TO BE ENDOWED WITH "THE SPIRIT OF THEIR LEADER", COUPLED WITH "ASTUTENESS" AND "BUSINESS ACUMEN" WHICH CAUSES THEM TO HAVE:

*THE COURAGE OF JOSHUA
* THE "BULLDOG" TENACITY OF SAMPSON
* THE "SPIRIT TO PROTECT AND SERVE"
LIKE AARON AND HUR
*THE WISDOM OF SOLOMON

*"If any of you lack wisdom,
let him ask of God, that giveth to all men
liberally, and upbraideth not;
and it shall be given him."
James 1:5 KJV*

78

"And he sighed deeply in his spirit, and saith, Why doth this generation seek after a sign?"
Mark 8:12a KJV

"For the Jews require a sign, and the Greeks seek after wisdom: but we preach Christ crucified, unto the Jews a stumblingblock, and unto the Greeks foolishness;"
1 Corinthians 1:22-23 KJV

THE WORLD LOOKS FOR A BIGN. THEREFORE; PARTICIPATION IN CHRISTENDOM AS WELL AS IN CHURCHDOM IS PREDICATED. GREATLY UPON "SIGNS". GOD IS MOVING HEAVILY IN THEOPHANY - "THE VISIBLE MANIFESTATION OF GOD" GET READY FOR AN "EPIPHANY MOMENT" IN YOUR LIFE AND FAMILY".
MIRACLES, SIGNS, AND WONDERS

"Let your light so shine before men, that they may see your good works, and glorify your Father which is in heaven."
Matthew 5:16 KJV
BE HEALED, BE DELIVERED; BE SET FREE!

You are that sign and that "catalyst" that God will use mightily in this generation to "speed up the reaction" for many to be won into the KINGDOM OF GOD!

AN "APOSTLE"
IS BY DEFINITION -
"ONE SENT ON A MISSION";
THEREFORE:
HIS DESIGNATION - "THE SENT ONE"
HIS SCOPE - "TO THE NATIONS"

"BUT THE LORD SAID UNTO ME, SAY NOT, I AM A CHILD: FOR THOU SHALT GO TO ALL THAT I SHALL SEND THEE, AND WHATSOEVER I COMMAND THEE THOU SHALT SPEAK. SEE, I HAVE THIS DAY SET THEE OVER THE NATIONS AND OVER THE KINGDOMS, TO ROOT OUT, AND TO PULL DOWN, AND TO DESTROY, AND TO THROW DOWN, TO BUILD, AND TO PLANT."

JEREMIAH 1:7, 10 KJV

THERE CAN BE, ABSOLUTELY, NO "NAROW-MINDEDNESS" OR "TUNNEL-VISION", IN YOUR QUEST TO EXPAND GLOBALLY.

STOP SAYING, "MY CHURCH (MY REFORMATION) IS INDEPENDENT". DON'T ISOLATE YOURSELF ON AN ISLAND OF LONELINESS. YOUR VISION WILL MANIFEST QUICKER THROUGH "APOSTOLIC CONNECTIVITY". JOIN THE RANKS OF THOSE, OF US, WHO EMBRACE "KOINONIA - GENUINE FELLOWSHIP" AND ENCOURAGE OTHERS TO DO THE SAME.

IN THE WORDS OF JOHN DONNE, "NO MAN IS AN ISLAND".

"GOD WILL GIVE YOU AS FAR AS YOU CAN SEE"

"Simon Peter, a servant and an apostle of Jesus Christ, to them that have obtained like precious faith with us through the righteousness of God and our Saviour Jesus Christ: grace and peace be multiplied unto you through the knowledge of God, and of Jesus our Lord, according as his divine power hath given unto us all things that pertain unto life and godliness, through the knowledge of him that hath called us to glory and virtue: whereby are given unto us exceeding great and precious promises: that by these ye might be partakers of the divine nature, having escaped the corruption that is in the world through lust. And beside this, giving all diligence, add to your faith virtue; and to virtue knowledge; and to knowledge temperance; and to temperance patience; and to patience godliness; and to godliness brotherly kindness; and to brotherly kindness charity. For if these things be in you, and abound, they make you that ye shall neither be barren nor unfruitful in the knowledge of our Lord Jesus Christ. But he that lacketh these things is blind, and cannot see afar off, and hath forgotten that he was purged from his old sins. Wherefore the rather, brethren, give diligence to make your calling and election sure: for if ye do these things, ye shall never fall: for so an entrance shall be ministered unto you abundantly into the everlasting kingdom of our Lord and Saviour Jesus Christ. Wherefore I will not be negligent to put you always in remembrance of these things, though ye know them, and be established in the present truth. Yea, I think it meet, as long as I am in this tabernacle, to stir you up by putting you in remembrance; knowing that shortly I must put off this my tabernacle, even as our Lord Jesus Christ hath shewed me. Moreover I will endeavour that ye may be able after my decease to have these things always in remembrance. For we have not followed cunningly devised fables, when we made known unto you the power and coming of our Lord Jesus Christ, but were eyewitnesses of his majesty. For he received from God the Father honour and glory, when there came such a voice to him from the excellent glory, This is my beloved Son, in whom I am well pleased. And this voice which came from heaven we heard, when we were with him in the holy mount. We have also a more sure word of prophecy; whereunto ye do well that ye take heed, as unto a light that shineth in a dark place, until

the day dawn, and the day star arise in your hearts: knowing this first, that no prophecy of the scripture is of any private interpretation. For the prophecy came not in old time by the will of man: but holy men of God spake as they were moved by the Holy Ghost."
2 Peter 1:1-21 KJV

AS YOU ENTER INTO COVENANT WITH A "LOCAL CHURCH" OR AN "INTERNATIONAL REFORMATION" IT IS ENCUMBERED UPON YOU TO "MAKE YOUR CALLING AND ELECTION SURE." IF YOU FAIL TO DO THIS, YOU GIVE PLACE TO THE DEVIL TO ABORT YOUR MINISTRY AND; SUBSEQUENTLY, YOUR LIFE.

Daniel 11:32-33a KJV
"And such as do wickedly against the covenant shall he corrupt by flatteries: but the people that do know their God shall be strong, and do exploits. And they that understand among the people shall instruct many:"

Ephesians 4:25-29
"Wherefore putting away lying, speak every man truth with his neighbour: for we are members one of another. Be ye angry, and sin not: let not the sun go down upon your wrath: neither give place to the devil. Let him that stole steal no more: but rather let him labour, working with his hands the thing which is good, that he may have to give to him that needeth. Let no corrupt communication proceed out of your mouth, but that which is good to the use of edifying, that it may minister grace unto the hearers."

THE DEVIL IS THE FATHER OF LIES; AND HE IS THE CHIEF SOOTHSAYER, WHO HAS HIS GENERALS STRATEGICALLY AND TERRITORIALLY LOCATED, WITH THEIR BARKING HELLHOUNDS.THEREFORE. I IMPLORE YOU TO NOT BE VICTIMIZED BY ANY IOTA OF DEMONISM:

"O foolish Galatians, who hath bewitched you, that ye should not obey the truth, before whose eyes Jesus Christ hath been evidently set forth, crucified among you?"
Galatians 3:1 KJV

66 *And Samuel said to Saul, Thou hast done foolishly: thou hast not kept the commandment of the LORD thy God, which he commanded thee: for now would the LORD have established thy kingdom upon Israel forever. But now thy kingdom shall not continue: the LORD hath sought him a man after his own heart, and the LORD hath commanded him to be captain over his people, because thou hast not kept that which the LORD commanded thee."*
1 Samuel 13:13-14 KJV

> KING DAVID WAS THAT MAN WHOM THE LORD SOUGHT ("A" MAN AFTER HIS OWN HEART).
>
> NOTICE THE FACT THAT GOD DID NOT SEEK DAVID TO BE "THE" Man, BUT "A" MAN AFTER HIS OWN HEART; THIS SIGNIFIES THE FACTUAL TRUTH THAT GOD IS STILL SEEKING FOR MEN (WOMEN) TO JOIN THE RANKS OF THIS ELEVATION.
> I AM ON MY QUEST FOR THE SAME; WON'T YOU JOIN ME IN YOUR QUEST? BE REMINDED IN THE PROCESS THAT:

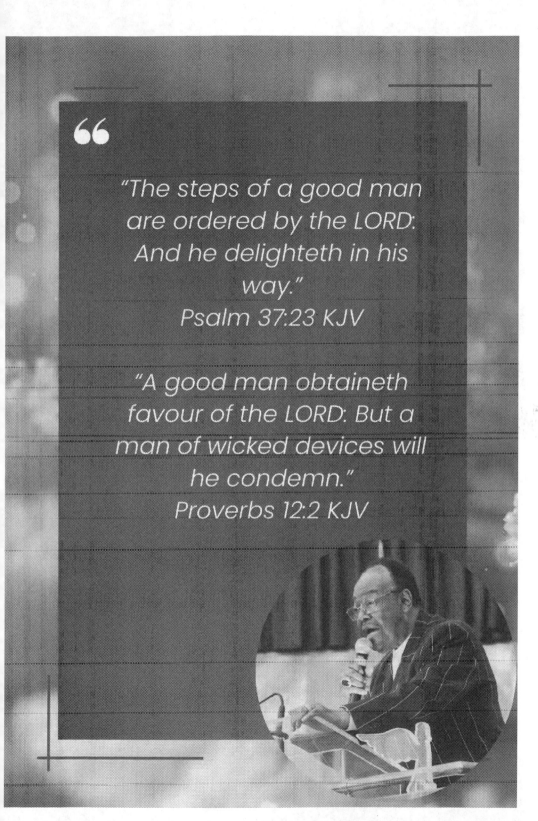

"The steps of a good man
are ordered by the LORD:
And he delighteth in his
way."
Psalm 37:23 KJV

"A good man obtaineth
favour of the LORD: But a
man of wicked devices will
he condemn."
Proverbs 12:2 KJV

"EVERYTHING THAT I KNOW IS TRYING TO LIVE; NOT SUCCUMB TO SUICIDAL TENDENCIES!"

IN MY STUDIES OF BIOLOGY, EVEN THE PLANTS AND ANIMALS (EVERY SPECIES THEREOF), NEVER CEASE TO STRIVE FOR LIFE; THEREFORE, DOES IT NOT STAND TO REASON THAT WE, AS HOMOSAPIENS ("GOD-GIVEN HUMANKIND") SHOULD HONOR THE QUEST FOR LIFE. IN CHRISTENDOM AND CHURCHDOM, WE NOT ONLY STRIVE FOR LIFE BUT MASTERY (DOMINION, ASCENDANCY - THE UPPER HAND IN COMPETITION); THATS HUMAN-NATURE; AND YET WE ARE BIBLICALLY CHARGED IN OUR QUEST:

"Thou therefore endure hardness, as a good soldier of Jesus Christ. No man that warreth entangleth himself with the affairs of this life; that he may please him who hath chosen him to be a soldier. And if a man also strive for masteries, yet is he not crowned, except he strive lawfully."
2 Timothy 2:3-5 KJV

STRIVE
SURVIVE
LIVE

WHEN WE GIVE FAITHFULLY AND
CONSISTENTLY "AS UNTO THE
LORD" (NOT MAN), WE ARE
BLESSEDLY ENDEAVORING TO DULY
GIVE BACK TO HIM A MERE
PORTION OF THAT, THAT HE HAS
GIVEN UNTO US.

"Give, and it shall be given unto you;
good measure, pressed down, and
shaken together, and running over,
shall men give into your bosom. For
with the same measure that ye mete
withal it shall be measured to you
again." -Luke 6:38 KJV

FREELY GIVE YOUR
TIME
FREELY GIVE YOUR
TALENT
FREELY GIVE YOUR
TITHE

"THE KING IS COMING"

"And in the sixth month the angel Gabriel was sent from God unto a city of Galilee, named Nazareth, To a virgin espoused to a man whose name was Joseph, of the house of David; and the virgin's name was Mary. And the angel came in unto her, and said, Hail, thou that art highly favoured, the Lord is with thee: blessed art thou among women. And when she saw him, she was troubled at his saying, and cast in her mind what manner of salutation this should be. And the angel said unto her, Fear not, Mary: for thou hast found favour with God. And, behold, thou shalt conceive in thy womb, and

bring forth a son, and shalt call his name JESUS. He shall be great, and shall be called the Son of the Highest: and the Lord God shall give unto him the throne of his father David: And he shall reign over the house of Jacob for ever; and of his kingdom there shall be no end. Then said Mary unto the angel, How shall this be, seeing I know not a man? And the angel answered and said unto her, The Holy Ghost shall come upon thee, and the power of the Highest shall overshadow thee: therefore also that holy thing which shall be born of thee shall be called the Son of God."
Luke 1:26-35 KJV

Over 700 years prior to this angelic prophecy, the Lord had spoken to the major prophet Isaiah:

"For unto us a child is born, unto us a son is given: and the government* shall be upon his shoulder: and his name shall be called Wonderful, Counsellor, The mighty God, The everlasting Father, The Prince of Peace. Of the increase of his government and peace there shall be no end, upon the throne of David, and upon his kingdom, to order it, and to establish it with judgment and with justice from henceforth even for ever.

The zeal of the Lord of hosts will perform this."
Isaiah 9:6-7 KJ

*government-authoritative control"

THERE HAD BEEN PRIOR GOVERNMENTS FOR GOD'S CHOSEN PEOPLE, BUT IT IS MADE CLEAR THAT "OF THE INCREASE OF HIS GOVERNMENT AND PEACE THERE SHALL BE NO END"

What God decrees no man can stop it!

If the Red Sea couldn't stop Moses,
If the Jericho Wall couldn't stop Joshua,
If the giant Goliath couldn't stop David;
If death couldn't stop Jesus,
Then, nothing can stop God from giving an angel charge over Mary for the safe delivery of Jesus, the king of kings.

LOOK AT THE HISTORICITY OF GOD'S CHOSEN PEOPLE

1.) From the fall of Adam the earth was corrupt, families (the first institution of God) were corrupt, worship was corrupt and every man "did that which was right in his own eyesight," until God completely wiped man off the surface of the earth with a flood. But God found grace in Noah, who built the ark, whom He made a covenant with...from the lineage of Adam through Seth signified by a rainbow in the sky.

"NO MORE WATER BUT FIRE NEXT TIME"

Abraham became the "father of the faithful whom God could entrust with prosperity and His chosen people. His son, Isaac passed the blessing on to Jacob...twelve tribes Israel (name change - "a prince with God".)

THEN WE BEHOLD GOD'S CHOSEN PEOPLE IN EGYPTIAN BONDAGE...AND THEIR DELIVERANCE AFTER 400 YEARS THROUGH MOSES.

This ushered in the second(2) God-ordained institution known as Civil Government wherein God sent His laws statutes, judgments, and ordinances through His leader, Moses, and "they could not keep a single one of them."

Then He allowed judges to rule over Israel to seek to reconcile the family as well as the land to himself...fifteen judges reigned from Othniel to Samuel which included Gideon, Sampson, and Deborah the only female.

Then Israel asked God for a
king to reign over them; God
allowed Saul to be the first
king...followed by David and
Solomon. Each one of them
reigned for 40 years. There
was a total of 43 kings and
one queen, Athaliah. Israelic
kingship ends in 597 b.c.
when Israel is captured by
Babylonian King
Nebuchadnezzar.

God so loved His people that
He sent priests and prophets
while the Kings were
reigning.

Yet, God's chosen people continued to go down the corridor of apostasy; into a cesspool of idolatry. They remained in Babylonian captivity for 70 years.

THE HEAVENS WERE SHUT UP FOR 400 YEARS. (FROM MALACHI TO ST. MATTHEW)

2.) Then God saw the need to reconcile...redeem man back to himself.

THE PROPHETS HAD PROPHESIED RIGHTEOUSLY AND GOD WAS NOT ABOUT TO LET HIS WORD RETURN UNTO HIM VOID:

Isaiah (silver-tongued, eagle-eyed prophet) had prophesied extensively that there would be hope for the land...families...God's chosen people:

"For unto us a child is born, unto us a son is given: and the government shall be upon his shoulder: and his name shall be called Wonderful, Counsellor, The mighty God, The everlasting Father, The Prince of Peace." Isaiah 9:6 KJV

So it is, we see the triune counsel as they convened. The Heavens were searched, the earth was searched and no man was found worthy to fulfill the mission.

Then Jesus said, "Prepare me a body and I'll go down...I'll take off this Royal robe long enough to make sure that the land...The Family Institution and all who believe will have a chance"...through the second-man, Adam.

...so it is:

"For God so loved the world, that he gave his only begotten Son, that whosoever believeth in him should not perish, but have everlasting life. For God sent not his Son into the world to condemn the world; but that the world through him might be saved. He that believeth on him is not condemned: but he that believeth not is condemned already, because he hath not believed in the name of the only begotten Son of God."
John 3:16-18 KJV

"Then said he, Lo, I come to do thy will, O God. He taketh away the first, that he may establish the second. By the which will we are sanctified through the offering of the body of Jesus Christ once for all. And every priest standeth daily ministering and offering oftentimes the same sacrifices, which can never take away sins: But this man, after he had offered one sacrifice for sins for ever, sat down on the right hand of God;

From henceforth expecting till his enemies be made his footstool. For by one offering he hath perfected for ever them that are sanctified."
Hebrews 10:9-14 KJV

...came down through 42 generations...born of a virgin, Mary, through the seed of the Holy Ghost...

JUST AS MARY HAD AN IMMACULATE CONCEPTION THROUGH THE HOLY GHOST, WE CAN RECEIVE JESUS TODAY TO DWELL WITHIN US THROUGH THE EMPOWERMENT OF THE HOLY GHOST...

From henceforth expecting till his enemies be made his footstool. For by one offering he hath perfected for ever them that are sanctified."
Hebrews 10:9-14 KJV

...came down through 42 generations...born of a virgin, Mary, through the seed of the Holy Ghost...

JUST AS MARY HAD AN IMMACULATE CONCEPTION THROUGH THE HOLY GHOST, WE CAN RECEIVE JESUS TODAY TO DWELL WITHIN US THROUGH THE EMPOWERMENT OF THE HOLY GHOST...

EVEN SO, COME, LORD JESUS...

3,) As we embrace this season let us remember that life is filled with swift transitions. We experience many mundane vicissitudes and proclivities while traveling here as pilgrims and sojourners.

IF WE ARE GOING TO RECEIVE THIS AMAZING GRACE, WE MUST BELIEVE THE REPORT THAT JESUS SAVES AND HIS BLOOD WASHES WHITER THAN SNOW. (I CHOOSE TO BELIEVE THE REPORT).

David declared in Psalms 24:6-10

This is the generation of them that seek him, that seek thy face, O Jacob. Selah. Lift up your heads, O ye gates; and be ye lift up, ye everlasting doors; and the King of glory shall come in. Who is this King of glory? The Lord strong and mighty, the Lord mighty in battle. Lift up your heads, O ye gates; even lift them up, ye everlasting doors; and the King of glory shall come in. Who is this King of glory? The Lord of hosts, he is the King of glory. Selah.

(Psalms 24:6-10 KJV)

HE IS THE ONE WHO COMES TO BRING THE FULLNESS OF AMAZING GRACE:

King Solomon posed a prophetic question:

Who is this that cometh out of the wilderness like pillars of smoke, perfumed with myrrh and frankincense, with all powders of the merchant?
(Song of Solomon 3:6 KJV)

Isaiah, the silver-tongued prophet; the eagle-eyed prophet saw him over 700 years before his coming:

WE ARE CONTINUOUSLY DECLARING BUT:

Who hath believed our report? and to whom is the arm of the Lord revealed? For he shall grow up before him as a tender plant, and as a root out of a dry ground: he hath no form nor comeliness; and when we shall see him, there is no beauty that we should desire him. He is despised and rejected of men; a man of sorrows, and acquainted with grief: and we hid as it were our faces from him; he was despised, and we esteemed him not. Surely he hath borne our griefs, and carried our sorrows: yet we did esteem him stricken, smitten of God, and afflicted. But he was wounded for our transgressions, he was bruised for our iniquities: the chastisement of our peace was upon him, and with his stripes, we are healed.

WE ARE HEALED, DELIVERED, SET FREE:

-FROM EVERY "MIND-BOGGLING", "SPIRIT-STIFFLING", BODY-DETEORATING" ASPECT OF THE ENEMY.

WE ARE JUSTIFIED (MADE RIGHT AS THOUGH WE HAVE NEVER BEEN WRONG)

WE ARE SANCTIFIED (CLEANSED AND MADE FIT FOR THE MASTER'S USE)

WE ARE EMPOWERED WITH THE ANOINTED KEEPING POWER OF THE HOLY GHOST.

THERE IS A SHIFT FROM DISGRACE TO AMAZING GRACE.

THE APOSTLE IS
ARDENTLY AND
DEFINITIVELY
"NON-SELF-
SERVING".
HE IS
CATEGORICALLY,
PRECEDENTLY,
AND
UNRELENTINGLY -
"A SERVANT-
LEADER".

THE APOSTLE IS PURPOSELY
DESTINED, BY THE GRACE OF
GOD, TO "REACH THE MASSES"
AND EFFECT CHANGE THAT
DELIVERS FROM:

- FRAGMENTATION TO
  WHOLENESS
- SICKNESS TO WELLNESS
- ILLITERACY TO LITERACY
- FEAR TO BOLDNESS
- DOUBT TO FAITH
- DAMNATION TO SALVATION
- DISGRACE TO "AMAZING
  GRACE"

...AND A PLETHORA OF
CATEGORIES AS NEEDED.

PLEASE PARTICIPATE IN THE
PROCESS OF "REACHING THE
LOST AT ANY COST THROUGH
PENTECOST".

DISCERNING THE LORD'S BODY...

"For as often as ye eat this bread, and drink this cup, ye do shew the Lord's death till he come. Wherefore whosoever shall eat this bread, and drink this cup of the Lord, unworthily, shall be guilty of the body and blood of the Lord. But let a man examine himself, and so let him eat of that bread, and drink of that cup. For he that eateth and drinketh unworthily, eateth and drinketh damnation to himself,

not discerning the Lord's body.
For this cause many are weak
and sickly among you, and many
sleep. For if we would judge
ourselves, we should not be
judged. But when we are judged,
we are chastened of the Lord,
that we should not be
condemned with the world."
1 Corinthians 11:26-32 KJV

not discerning the Lord's body. For this cause many are weak and sickly among you, and many sleep. For if we would judge ourselves, we should not be judged. But when we are judged, we are chastened of the Lord, that we should not be condemned with the world."
1 Corinthians 11:26-32 KJV

DISCERN -
to detect with the eyes,
to detect with senses other than
vision, to come to know or
recognize mentally

THE LORD'S BODY - His church
CHURCH - "body" of baptized
believers in CHRIST

**"WHEREFORE, TO DISCERN HIS BODY
IS TO DISCERN HIS CHURCH"; TO
DISCERN HIS CHURCH IS TO
RECOGNIZE, FACTUALLY, THAT THE
CHURCH IS HIS BODY, WHICH IS
DISCERNIBLE."**

THEREFORE, WE SHOULD RECOGNIZE, FURTHER, THAT:

"Wherefore he saith, When he ascended up on high, he led captivity captive, And gave gifts unto men." Ephesians 4:8 KJV

...HE GAVE GIFTS TO MEN; NOT ANGELS

...HE GAVE GIFTS TO HIS CHURCH - "HIS BODY (BAPTIZED BELIEVERS IN CHRIST.

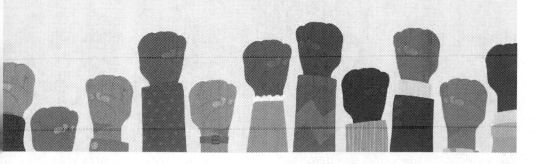

- GIFTS:
"And he gave some, apostles;
and some, prophets; and some,
evangelists; and some, pastors
and teachers; for the perfecting
of the saints, for the work of the
ministry, for the edifying of the
body of Christ: till we all come in
the unity of the faith, and of the
knowledge of the Son of God,
unto a perfect man, unto the
measure of the stature of the
fulness of Christ: that we
henceforth be no more children,
tossed to and fro, and carried

about with every wind of doctrine, by the sleight of men, and cunning craftiness, whereby they lie in wait to deceive; but speaking the truth in love, may grow up into him in all things, which is the head, even Christ: from whom the whole body fitly joined together and compacted by that which every joint supplieth, according to the effectual working in the measure of every part, maketh increase of the body unto the edifying of itself in love."
Ephesians 4:11-16 KJV

about with every wind of doctrine, by the sleight of men, and cunning craftiness, whereby they lie in wait to deceive; but speaking the truth in love, may grow up into him in all things, which is the head, even Christ: from whom the whole body fitly joined together and compacted by that which every joint supplieth, according to the effectual working in the measure of every part, maketh increase of the body unto the edifying of itself in love."
Ephesians 4:11-16 KJV

- GIFTS...

"Now there are diversities of gifts, but the same Spirit. And there are differences of administrations, but the same Lord. And there are diversities of operations, but it is the same God which worketh all in all. But the manifestation of the Spirit is given to every man to profit withal. For to one is given by the Spirit the word of wisdom; to another the word of knowledge by the same Spirit; to another faith by the same Spirit;

to another the gifts of healing by the same Spirit; to another the working of miracles; to another prophecy; to another discerning of spirits; to another divers kinds of tongues; to another the interpretation of tongues: but all these worketh that one and the selfsame Spirit, dividing to every man severally as he will.

For as the body is one, and hath many members, and all the members of that one body, being many, are one body: so also is Christ. For by one Spirit are we all baptized into one body, whether we be Jews or Gentiles, whether we be bond or free; and have been all made to drink into one Spirit. For the body is not one member, but many. If the foot shall say, Because I am not the hand, I am not of the body; is it therefore not of the body?

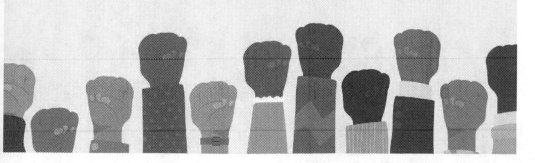

And if the ear shall say, Because I am not the eye, I am not of the body; is it therefore not of the body? If the whole body were an eye, where were the hearing? If the whole were hearing, where were the smelling? But now hath God set the members every one of them in the body, as it hath pleased him. And if they were all one member, where were the body? But now are they many members, yet but one body. And the eye cannot say unto the hand, I have no need of thee:

nor again the head to the feet, I have no need of you. Nay, much more those members of the body, which seem to be more feeble, are necessary: and those members of the body, which we think to be less honourable, upon these we bestow more abundant honour; and our uncomely parts have more abundant comeliness. For our comely parts have no need: but God hath tempered the body together, having given more abundant honour to that part

which lacked: that there should be no schism in the body; but that the members should have the same care one for another. And whether one member suffer, all the members suffer with it; or one member be honoured, all the members rejoice with it. Now ye are the body of Christ, and members in particular. And God hath set some in the church, first apostles, secondarily prophets, thirdly teachers, after that miracles, then gifts of

healings, helps, governments, diversities of tongues. Are all apostles? are all prophets? are all teachers? are all workers of miracles? Have all the gifts of healing? do all speak with tongues? do all interpret? But covet earnestly the best gifts: and yet shew I unto you a more excellent way." 1 Corinthians 12:4-31 KJV

THEREFORE, WE MUST CONCLUDE THAT, WHEN WE DISCERN THE LORD'S BODY, WE ARE DISCERNING HIS CHURCH - HIS BODY OF BAPTIZED BELIEVERS WHO ARE "GIFTED AND ANOINTED:

"For he that eateth and drinketh unworthily, eateth and drinketh damnation to himself, not discerning the Lord's body. For this cause many are weak and sickly among you, and many sleep. For if we would judge ourselves, we should not be judged. But when we are judged,

we are chastened of the Lord, that we should not be condemned with the world."
1 Corinthians 11:29-32 KJV

...STOP JUDGING "GOD'S ANOINTED GIFTS" TO HIS BODY, DISCERN HIS BODY; JUDGE YOURSELF
...DISCERN HIS BODY RIGHTEOUSLY
...QUIT BEING INTIMIDATED BY "MINISTRY-GIFTS"
...CELEBRATE EACH OTHER

"LET US MAKE MAN"...

THERE ARE THOSE GAIN-SAYERS, NAY-SAYERS, DOOM-SAYERS, AND EVEN, SOOTHSAYERS WHO COLLABORATE AND CORROBORATE "VICIOUSLY" AGAINST THE ELEVATION OF YOUNG MEN, ESPECIALLY. BUT I CAN SEE GOD AS HE CALLED HIS "GOD-HEAD" TRIBUNAL INTO SESSION:

"AND GOD SAID, LET US MAKE MAN IN OUR IMAGE, AFTER OUR LIKENESS: AND LET THEM HAVE DOMINION OVER THE FISH OF THE SEA, AND OVER THE FOWL OF THE AIR, AND OVER THE CATTLE, AND OVER ALL THE EARTH, AND OVER EVERY CREEPING THING THAT CREEPETH UPON THE EARTH."

GENESIS 1:26

APOSTLES DO NOT BELITTLE OR CONTEND AGAINST THE ORDINANCE OF GOD, WE CELEBRATE IT"

IN THIS CHURCH AGE WHEREIN THE CHURCH HAS BEEN EMPOWERED WITH HOLY SPIRIT, LET US NOT FAIL TO USE THIS DIVINE KINGDOM SOURCE OF GUIDANCE.

THE HOLY SPIRIT IS OUR PARACLETE (HELPER) AS WE FORGE AHEAD IN DIVINE KINGDOM ORDER WITH:

"THE MAKING OF MEN WITHIN THE BODY OF CHRIST"

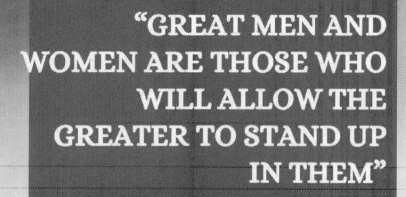

"GREAT MEN AND WOMEN ARE THOSE WHO WILL ALLOW THE GREATER TO STAND UP IN THEM"

"Ye are of God, little children, and have overcome them: because greater is he that is in you than he that is in the world."
1 John 4:4 KJV

GUARDING THE HEART OF THE APOSTLE...

The apostle must conduct himself in a spirit that is marinated with:
CALMNESS + SERENITY + TRANQUILITY = PEACE

"And the peace of God, which passeth all understanding, shall keep your hearts and minds through Christ Jesus."
Philippians 4:7 KJV

THEREFORE, TO ASSURE THAT PEACE, HE MUST CIRCUMFERENCE {SURROUND) HIMSELF WITH A "CADRE" OF GODLY "SOLDIERS OF THE CROSS AND FOLLOWERS OF THE LAMB" WHO ARE COMMITTED, WHOLEHEARTEDLY, TO "GUARD HIS HEART";

CADRE - a nucleus or core group especially of trained personnel able to assume control and; thusly, train others. - a group of people having some unifying relationship.

THAT IS CONCLUSIVELY, "THE HEART OF THE MATTER". THE TRUE VINE CHURCHES OF DELIVERANCE (TVCOD), DEFINITELY, HAS A UNIFYING RELATIONSHIP:

TVCOD - A SYSTEMIC NETWORK OF JURISDICTIONAL CHURCHES IN COVENANT FELLOWSHIP. "COME OVER MACEDONIA AND HELP US"

"And a vision appeared to Paul in the night; There stood a man of Macedonia, and prayed him, saying, Come over into Macedonia, and help us."
Acts 16:9 KJV

THE APOSTOLIC DOXOLOGY:

"Praise God from whom all blessings flow,
Praise Him all creatures here below,
Praise Him above ye heavenly host,
Praise Father, Son, and Holy Ghost."

"Praise God, from Whom All Blessings Flow"
by Thomas Ken
The United Methodist Hymnal, 95

THE APOSTOLIC BENEDICTION:

"Now unto him that is able to do exceeding abundantly above all that we ask or think, according to the power that worketh in us,"
Ephesians 3:20 KJV

About the Author
APOSTLE DR. SYLVESTER DAVIS JOHNSON

Apostle Sylvester Davis Johnson is an internationally known and much sought-after preacher, teacher, singer, musician, and author. He is noted for his humility as a servant of the Lord. Recognized as having a call to nurture, train, and mentor spiritual sons, daughters, and pastors of new as well as established ministries, he has become the Apostolic covering of many. Apostle Johnson was listed as a member of the National Register's Who's Who in Executive and Professionals 2004-2005 Edition.

Reared in the home of a Bishop, the late Bishop William Monroe Johnson, and Mother Marie Davis Johnson recognized the church as his mainstay and was converted at the age of ten (10) years old. He is a "life member" and serves as the Senior Pastor of the Macedonia True Vine Pentecostal Holiness Church of God, Incorporated, Winston-Salem, North Carolina, currently, the Macedonia Worship Center. He is the Most Apostolic Primate/Establishmentarian of the True Vine Churches of Deliverance International (TVCOD) and serves as the Jurisdictional Presiding Prelate of the Greater Memorial Ecclesiastical Jurisdiction of TVCOD.
Under his capable leadership, after succeeding his father, the local church has experienced tremendous growth.

Printed in the United States
by Baker & Taylor Publisher Services